To be a Friend

SELECTED BY
BARBARA SHOOK HAZEN

THE C.R. GIBSON COMPANY, NORWALK, CONNECTICUT

*Friendship is born at the moment
when one person says to another
"What! You too? I thought
that no one but myself . . ."*

C. S. LEWIS

TRIBUTE TO A DEAR FRIEND

A real and dear friend
Is a rare, precious blend
Of rapport, understanding, and trust;
Who knows of our tears
And our joys through the years,
With whom all our plans are discussed;

Dear friends are those
Who never disclose
The dreams we entrust to their keeping;
They watch through the night
Till the morning's first light—
While others care not, and are sleeping;

Dear friends never change,
We never feel strange
But always at home when they're near;
Friendships like these
Make fond memories
Which just grow increasingly dear;

Their worth can't be told
In silver or gold,
For love can't be measured on charts;
They've a most special place
Which time can't erase
In that one certain spot in our hearts!

KATHERINE NELSON DAVIS

FRIENDS ARE FOR THE BEST OF TIMES

. . . especially when they are lifelong friends and you really enjoy each other and can't wait to catch up. Dorothy Van Doren, wife of the late poet-professor, Mark Van Doren, speaks from the heart as she speaks of friends. For her, as for so many of us, familiar faces breed loving times, which are the best of times.

A while ago my husband and I made a trip to San Francisco. We spent the night with a couple we have known for more than thirty years, the man having been a student of my husband's. We used to see them often, regularly in New York and every summer when they were our nearest neighbors in Connecticut; but in the last ten, maybe fifteen years, since they moved west, I don't believe I have seen either of them half a dozen times.

The visit was a great success. We found we had lots to talk about, not only to catch up with our respective lives since we had seen each other, but in general, about all sorts of subjects, on which as we used to do we more or less agreed. We were still talking busily when it was time to go to bed and we kept coming out of our bedrooms for another remark; finally we were all four out in the hall in various stages of undress, still talking sixteen to the dozen.

In the morning I asked the wife how they liked living in San Francisco. It was a beautiful city, she said, and that was plain to see; they had met some agreeable people; they enjoyed the climate, the view of the Bay, the cosmopolitan character of the place. "It's very nice to live in really," she said. "Only of course there are no old friends. At our age you don't make friends the way you used to; there isn't time."

I have often thought of what she said. Old friends. Among our own friends are a number I knew in college or met soon after; a greater number we both met during our first New York jobs, all this being some four decades ago. We still see them, not as often as we did surely, but in any sort of exceptional situation, good or bad; if my husband receives an honor for instance or if we go through a period of strain and difficulty, we hear from them. They don't necessarily say much when they write or telephone.

Quite often they simply send us their love.

We have lived long enough in our Connecticut town to have old friends, too. People we met the magic winter of our first sabbatical leave; people we got to know soon after. We sometimes get together with the sabbatical-winter friends and laugh about old times; the night the men got to playing chess and after a while they went outdoors and one of them said, "What's that light over there in the sky?" "That," replied another, "is the sun coming up." It was late winter, so the time was between six and seven in the morning. It was the time when our children were babies or small children; we look at our grandchildren now and remember those days with wry fondness. We remember square dances and evening picnics at the lake and going swimming by moonlight and getting stuck in the mud in the spring and things like that. We remember them together, because we have known each other for a long time. It would be hard, probably, for our younger friends whom we have not known so long to think of us doing the gay or foolish things they themselves do. We did them; and our old friends know it.

We went to a holiday party recently. It was a pleasant party and our hosts were old friends, too. But they have moved away and their guests were almost all strange to us. They were friendly people and easy to talk to, of course; but on the way home we said somehow the parties at home were more fun. People we see all the time, nothing new or surprising about them; we know when we can talk politics with them because they think as we do and when we can't unless we want to get into an exhausting and meaningless argument. We are likely to exchange gifts at Christmas and birthdays, gifts we have made ourselves maybe, some of us being much more clever than others at making things. It doesn't matter; it is the feeling of being old friends that matters.

Long ago some of our friends had a conversation about us which they later reported. We, they said, were among all their acquaintances the ones who most definitely had roots, who had stayed put, who could be counted on to be living in the same place next year or the year after. I was not sure then nor am I now that this is a good thing, but I expect it is true.

For us, we live the life we like. We like familiar objects, we like the same house. I go so far as to like the same way of placing furniture, but my children correct me on this. Most particularly we like the same friends; the ones we have known for quite a while. We like to get together with them at their houses or at our house, eat dinner, sit by the fire, and talk. We don't play bridge with them or canasta, we don't usually listen to music; we don't recite poetry or do charades (I hate charades). We just talk and after a while they go home or we do. I say it was a nice evening, wasn't it. A nice evening; rather a mild remark. But it was nice, it was pleasant, it was friendly. It was, indeed, full of love, unexpressed in ordinary times but in extraordinary times often clearly stated. In extraordinary times, in times of trouble, it is heart-moving to find how many old friends say they love you.

OLD FRIENDS

Old friends are true friends;
    Sunshine in the sky
Has kept us warm and fought the storm
    Through ages long gone by.

Sometimes the new friends
    Leave the heart aglow,
But it's when they're like the friends
    We cherished long ago.

PHILANDER JOHNSON

UNLIKELY FRIENDS

In her brilliant memoir, Lillian Hellman paints a pen portrait of her close friend, the great wit Dorothy Parker. Despite many dissimilarities, their friendship flourished.

I first met Dorothy Parker in 1931, shortly after I moved back to New York with Hammett. She caused a wacky-tipsy fight between us. She had read *The Maltese Falcon* and *Red Harvest*, perhaps a year or two before, and she had written about them, but she had not met Hammett until a cocktail party given by William Rose Benét. I was already uncomfortable at this party of people much older than myself, when a small, worn, prettyish woman was introduced to Hammett and immediately fell to her knees before him and kissed his hand. It was meant to be both funny and serious, but it was neither, and Hammett was embarrassed into a kind of simper.

That night I accused Dash of liking ladies who kissed his hand, he said I was crazy, I said I wasn't going to live with a man who allowed women to kneel in admiration, he said he had "allowed" no such thing, didn't like it.

I was not to meet Dottie again until the winter of 1935 in Hollywood, and then, having glared at her for most of the evening in memory of that silly first meeting, we talked. I liked her and we saw each other the next day and for many, many other good days and years until she died in June of 1967.

It was strange that we did like each other and that never through the years did two such difficult women ever have a quarrel, or even a mild, unpleasant word. Much, certainly, was against our friendship: we were not the same generation, we were not the same kind of writer, we had led and were to continue to lead very different lives, often we didn't like the same people or even the same books, but more important, we never liked the same men. When I met her in 1935 she was married to Alan Campbell, who was a hard man for me to take. He was also difficult for her and she would talk about him in a funny, half-bitter way not only to me but to a whole dinner party. But she had great affection for Alan and certainly—since she was to marry him twice—great dependence on him. If I didn't like Alan, she didn't like Hammett, although she was always too polite to say so. More important to me, Hammett, who seldom felt strongly about anybody, didn't like Dottie, and in the later years would move away from the house when she came to visit us.

I enjoyed her more than I have ever enjoyed any other woman. She was modest—this wasn't all virtue, she liked to think that she was not worth much—her view of people was original and sharp, her elaborate, overdelicate manners made her a pleasure to live with, she liked books and was generous about writers, and the wit, of course, was so wonderful that neither age nor illness ever dried up the spring from which it came fresh each day. No remembrance of her can exclude it.

But for me, the wit was never as attractive as the comment, often startling, always sudden, as if a curtain had opened and you had a brief and brilliant glance into what you would never have found for yourself. Like the wit, it was always delivered in a soft, clear voice; like the wit, it usually came after a silence, and started in the middle. One day she looked up from a book: "The man said he didn't want to see her again. That night she tried to climb into the transom of his hotel room and got stuck at the hips. I've never got stuck at the hips, Lilly, and I want you to remember that."

She was, more than usual, a tangled fishnet of contradictions.

THE FIX-UP

Popular writer, Judith Viorst, tells about "fixing up" her best friend with her husband's best friend. A natural thing for a friend to do? Maybe. Match-makers beware, and enjoy.

I have this friend Muriel who is attractive and intelligent and
    terribly understanding and loyal and
My husband has this friend Ralph who is handsome and witty
    and essentially very sincere and
Since they weren't engaged or even tactily committed
The least we could do, I said, is fix them up,
So I cooked this very nice boned chicken breasts with
    lemon-cream sauce and,
Put on a little Herb Alpert in the background and
Before Muriel came I told Ralph how she was attractive and
    intelligent and terribly understanding and loyal and
After Muriel came I drew out Ralph to show how he was
    witty and very sincere and
When dinner was over my husband and I did the dishes
Leaving Ralph and Muriel to get acquainted
With a little Petula Clark in the background and
We listened while they discovered that they both loved Mel
    Brooks and hated Los Angeles and agreed that the
    Supremes had lost their touch and
He insisted on taking her home even though she lived in the
    opposite direction and
The next day he phoned to ask is that what I call attractive,
    after which
She phoned to ask is that what I call sincere
And from now on
I cook lemon-cream sauce
For young marrieds.

FRIENDSHIP

If you're ever in a jam,
Here I am.
If you're ever in a mess,
S.O.S.
If you ever feel so happy you land in jail,
I'm your bail.
It's friendship, friendship,
Just a perfect blendship.
When other friendships have been forgot
Ours will still be hot.

COLE PORTER

WHAT FRIENDSHIP MEANS TO ME

To be a friend you have to care about people, what they think, what they feel, what they suffer. If you just don't like people, you may still be cordial to acquaintances, but friendship is no go. You must try to understand people, their hopes and fears and aspirations.

Friendship is a plant that has to be cultivated; it must be watered and tended if it is to produce sweet and wholesome fruit.

Friendship, to me, is an intangible thing, a kind of circle which completely surrounds another person taking him in with all his good points and all his bad, enveloping him in his entirety. If I come to like a man and a friendship is formed, it is because I have discerned something likable and lovable deep within him, something of character and fineness, although from time to time he may, as we all do, violate that which is fine and which is customarily a part of him. If he is my friend, there are two things I shall not think of doing: first, I shall not hurt him; second, I shall not cross him off my list because he was drunk or disorderly or thoughtless. To me it is cruel to criticize a friend in other than a light way. I prefer to leave criticism to his mere acquaintances. Inasmuch as they are not his friends they cannot hurt him.

To be a friend, in the deeper sense, may sometimes mean that you will be set down as an easy mark, a pushover. Most of the easy marks I have known have been a great deal happier than the smart little people who fool them. The fullest life is one that has contained the richest experiences, even though some of those experiences may have eventually led to disillusionment and to disappointment. A friend of mine once said, "I should rather believe in something and be wrong than not believe in it and be right." So with the man who has my friendship.

Friendship inevitably affects the body as well as the spirit. I doubt if it is possible to hate anybody and be completely healthy. Physicians agree that resentment fosters poison in the human system. It is not possible to love everybody, or even to like everybody, but at least, when there is no friendly response, the robe of tolerant indifference can be put on.

I am sure there are more good friends and good friendships in the world than we realize. From close observation of human beings I have come to the conclusion that the average person is better, not worse, than he seems to be. I have more than once discovered that men whom their fellows call selfish, ungenerous, hard, are almost daily engaged in the odds and ends of a thousand little kind and thoughtful acts. I have found many a soft conscience in a hard coat and many of the deeper qualities of friendship in an inarticulate man.

Above all, friendship means to me the immeasurable capacity for forgiveness. It means the ability to check off resentment, rather than let it persist and poison the spirit. Robert Louis Stevenson wrote, "He is a green hand at life who cannot forgive any mortal thing." There is no more enduring thing in life than real friendship. If it is not enduring, then it is not real, and has never quite found its way from the farflung fields of acquaintance to the inner circle of devotion.

GROVE PATTERSON

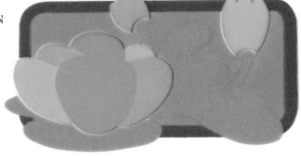

Time and measured miles don't matter to friends. It's inner distance that counts. The following two poems speak of the kind of closeness that survives separation.

WITH MY LOVE AS OF OLD

The roads we chose diverged so little at the setting-out and
    seemed so nearly side by side!
A little while we spoke across the way, then waved our hands,
    and then . . .
The hills between, life's other voices and the nights,
The silences . . .

Old friend, no new friend takes your place. With me as well
The hours and days flow by and lengthen into years,
But I do not forget. And not a thought that you have had of
    me—
Whether you wrote or spoke it, or, more like,
Just thought of me and let it go at that—
But it came winging through the silences!

Wherever you are, across the distance I give you my hand,
With my love as of old.

                                    JOHN PALMER GAVIT

ACROSS THE MILES

True friendship! with the thought appears
　Your jolly face, your happy smiles,
We may not meet for days or years
　But let's shake hands across the miles.

Yes, let's shake hands across the miles,
　The miles of sea, the miles of shore,
And trust the kindly afterwhiles
　May bring us face to face once more.

Though one may gaze on fields of snow,
　The other look on fields of green,
We're old-time comrades still, I know;
　No matter are the miles between.

The fates have lured us far apart,
　I miss you, and I miss your smiles,
But friendship holds us heart to heart,
　So let's shake hands across the miles.

JAMES BALL NAYLOR

HOW TO BE A COLLECTOR'S ITEM

Jean Kerr, playwright and humorist, wonders which of her friends will go down in the Hall of Fame, and worries that none of her friends will save her letters. The obvious solution: carbons. Here is her hilarious sneak peek at posterity.

I was reading another volume of collected letters last night, and it sent me right back to worrying about that old problem. On what basis do you decide that your friends are going to be famous, and that you ought to be saving their letters? Naturally, you save everything you get from Ernest Hemingway and Edith Sitwell. But think of the smart boys who were saving Edna Millay's penciled notes when she was just a slip of a thing at Vassar. What gets me is how they *knew.*

As sure as you're born, I'm tossing stuff into the wastebasket this minute that Scribner's would give their eyeteeth for twenty years from now. But you can't save *everybody's* letters, not in that five-room apartment. When I was young and naïve, last year, I used to file away mail if it seemed interesting or amusing. But that was a trap. For instance, I have a marvelous letter from my cleaning man explaining how he happened to break the coffee table. But clearly this is a one-shot affair. *He'll* never be collected. You have to use a little sense about these things.

No doubt the safest procedure is to confine yourself to those friends who have demonstrated a marked literary bent. Even then, I wouldn't collect anybody who didn't seem a good risk. If you have a friend who is a novelist, you might play it very close to the ground and wait until he wins a Pulitzer Prize. Of course, by that time he may not be writing to *you* any more.

If you have a friend who is a playwright, it's simpler. You begin collecting *him* immediately after his first failure. As letter writers, playwrights are at the top of their powers at this moment. For color, passion, and direct revelation of character you simply can't beat a letter from a playwright who has just had a four-day flop.

And sometimes you can see a talent bloom before your very eyes. I have one friend, a poet, who used to write nice little things about "the icy fingers of November" and "the strange stillness of ash trays after a party." I admit I didn't take him very seriously. But just last week he had a long poem in the *Partisan Review* and I didn't understand one word of it. Well, let me tell you, I'm saving his letters *now*.

You've got to keep your wits about you. It would be terrible to think you were brushing with greatness and didn't even notice. Oh, I'll admit there are times when you just can't be certain whether or not a friend has talent. In that case, just ask him. He'll tell you. But here, too, some discretion is necessary. For example, I don't give any serious attention to friends who get drunk at cocktail parties and announce they could write a better book than *Marjorie Morningstar*.

But who am I trying to fool with all this nonsense? Obviously, I'm not really worrying about my friends' letters. What keeps me awake nights is the question of my letters, the ones *I* write. Are they being saved? Fat chance. I know my friends—it simply wouldn't enter their scatterbrained heads that they ought to be collecting me. And poor Doubleday, how will they ever scrape together a book? Well, they won't, that's all, if I don't take steps.

So I'm taking steps. From now on I keep carbons of every word I write, and to hell with my cavalier pen-pals. I've got a very decent sampling already:

Dear Mabel,

Johnny doesn't seem to have a pair of socks without holes so tell him he has to wear one brown sock and one green sock. If he makes a fuss—tell him he can wear his long pants and they won't show. And another thing, very important—it's Gilbert's turn to drink his milk out of the beer mug.

Mrs. K.

Joan, dear—

Well, we finally moved into Hilltop and what a magical place it is! High, high above the slate-blue waters of the Bay. We have our very own special, sad, sighing wind. It seems enchanted and, we fancy, it is full of ghosts of Heathcliff and his Catherine. Promise you'll come and see us. We're always here.

Love,
Jean

The All-Season Window Corp.,
Mount Vernon, N.Y.
Dear Sirs,

Listen, are you going to come and put in those storm windows before we are blown out into the damn Sound? You said Monday and here it is Wednesday. We keep the thermostat up to eighty-five and still the toast is flying off the plates. And I had to put mittens on to type this.

I hope to hear from you soon or never.

Jean Kerr

Honey,

I seem to have lost my car key in Schrafft's so will you please take a cab and go pick up the car which I left in front of Bloomingdale's in New Rochelle? It's in a no-parking area but I don't think that matters because it's raining and Peggy says they never check in the rain. There are a lot of groceries on the back seat and I don't know what you're going to do with the ice cream.

Love, J.

Dear Chris,

Daddy and I are going out to supper and I want you to pay attention to this list.
1. No Disneyland until your homework is done.
2. Get your bicycle and all those guns out of the bathroom.
3. Take a bath and be sure to put one cup of Tide in the water.
4. Don't wear your underwear or your socks to bed.
5. Col says you swallowed his whistle. If you didn't, give it back to him.

Love, Mommy

Mr. Ken McCormick,
Doubleday & Co.,
New York, N.Y.
Dear Ken,

Thank you for saying the letters were interesting, and I shall, as you suggest, try Random House.

As always, Jean

P.S.: Will you kindly return this letter?

HEART FRIENDS

How generous is God that he has given me these few and special women who are the true friends of my heart.

How he must love me that he has let us find each other upon this crowded earth.

We are drawn to each other as if by some mystical force. We recognize each other at once. We are sisters of the spirit who understand each other instinctively.

There is no blood between us, no common family history. Yet there are no barriers of background, or even age. Older, younger, richer, poorer—no matter. We speak the same language, we have come together in a special moment of time, and the sense of union we feel will last throughout eternity.

How generous is God that he has given me so many other women I can call friends. Dear, good, life-enriching women who add flavor, value, delight. I would be the poorer without them.

Yet surely the Lord's true concern for us, his children, is to lead us to these rare and special few. The ones who call out to us from the crowds, who hold fast to us through trials, triumphs, long separations.

The friends with whom the heart feels joyfully at home.

MARJORIE HOLMES

True friends can share anything—
even a fear of the public eye.
In an intimate moment, the poet
Emily Dickinson allies herself
with someone who feels the same way.

I'm nobody! Who are you?
Are you nobody, too?
Then there's a pair of us—don't tell!
They'd banish us, you know.

How dreary to be somebody!
How public, like a frog
To tell your name the livelong day
To an admiring bog!

SOME FRIENDS ARE FOREVER

The time and miles between friends simply don't matter. Rob Wood reminisces about his childhood chum, Claudius, in a personal portrait. With Claudius, the writer first tasted turtle-egg soup and did a belly flop from a swinging vine. From Claudius, he learned all about watching jaybirds, winning and the importance of keeping score in your own head. Likely you'll recognize your best friend even if the name's not the same.

The first time I saw him was in early September, when the days have finished the slow, pleasant climb up the steep hill of summer and suddenly whiz downward at a terrifying speed toward the opening of school.

He leaned casually against a giant cottonwood, dressed in a muddy T-shirt and faded blue jeans, half cloth, half holes. A slingshot, obviously carved by a skilled young warrior, dangled from the one remaining hip pocket, and with his bare toes he picked up stones and sent them spinning, a talent that can be developed only after many shoeless months.

As the new boy in town, I studied him with the eyes of self-preservation, attempting to discover what form my indoctrination in this central Texas community would take—wrestling, fistfighting, foot racing or talking. While I squirmed with apprehension, he calmly watched a bird flutter into the cottonwood. He studied it intently, then turned to me with a grin that seemed to split his face in half. "Jaybird," he said. "Mighty pretty thing, but watch that old squawker when it's got a baby. Mean as hell."

With that he strolled over and squatted down a few yards in front of me. "I live over yonder," he said. "My name's Claudius. C-l-a-u-d-i-u-s. 'Fore you ask, my mother's a big 'un for reading books. That's where she got it—outta some book.

"The sun says it's two o'clock—way past dinnertime," he said. I glanced at my birthday wrist watch; the hands pointed to ten minutes after two. "Come on, we got some cold quail in the icebox."

To him, it was that simple. We were to be friends.

For the next six years, Claudius was to fill that one great need of childhood: to be able to point to someone and say, "Yonder's my best friend." To him, friendship was a pledge of loyalty and unselfishness, given without question or motive. He gladly shared his knowledge of the outdoors without the usual childhood bragging or intimidation. He taught me to fish for crawdads with a hunk of bacon and a bent pin, to name every wild flower on the hillsides, to swing from a vine over Little River and drop into the exact spot where the current would carry you downstream for a quarter of a mile and deposit you on the slippery, muddy bank.

On the day I was to try the vine-swinging act for the first time, my stomach churned with fear, and I couldn't move. Several playmates began to taunt: "Look there, he's scared to even try it." "You ain't getting yellow, are you?"

Claudius came up the muddy bank and stood next to me. He whispered, "It's just the getting around to doing that scares you, not the doing." He yelled down to those taunting me from the water, "Watch out below! We're going to do something that's never been done before. We're going to swing out on this one little vine together and then drop off. We dare any of you all to do it."

We swung with a belly-sinking arc over the water as the vine strained under our weight. We turned loose and drifted downward as if in one of those falling nightmares until we knifed through the water, bobbed to the surface, and spun downstream to the landing place. The others spread the word the next day of our daring.

With Claudius I tasted my first turtle-egg soup, first rabbit stew, first blackbird pie, and first bean-hole beans—a taste memory that still awakens me at night with a hunger that could only be sated with this culinary miracle of pinto beans, tomatoes, onions and bacon, cooked in a can buried deep in the ground over smoldering coals.

One lazy, nothing-to-do afternoon, conversation among a group of our classmates developed into a debate on the fighting ability of those attending the local grade school. Never especially strong, I did have tenacity, developed for no other reason than that my father was the high-school football coach in a football-crazy town. This alone made it necessary for me to defend my honor, and his, on many occasions, especially during losing seasons. Claudius had not been compelled to prove *his* worth since the day he was pushed into a fight with the largest boy in the class and had crushed the bully into the playground dust.

As the clamor for a showdown increased, I yielded to social pressure and announced that we'd settle it with a wrestling match, as best friends shouldn't fistfight. Claudius, who had been silent throughout the argument, rose slowly, peeled off his shirt, and said, "Let's go, but I still don't know why."

Three hours later, the contest was called a draw. Both of us were scratched, skinned, bloody, sweaty and grass-stained. Claudius turned toward home, while I listened to the praises of the hangers-on. Just once Claudius looked at me. With saddened eyes, he said softly, "Friends don't have to prove nothing to nobody, much less to each other."

As the passing years added a few grams of wisdom here and there, I realized that had he expended all his strength, the three-hour match would have ended in 15 minutes.

Claudius and I parted in our early teens when my family moved. We attempted to keep the friendship alive with summer visits, exchanges of Christmas gifts—mine generally purchased, his always a handmade wonder—and an occasional letter from me. "What can you tell a friend," he'd say, explaining why he never wrote, "by putting words down on paper and not even knowing if he understands what you mean?"

Then, one Thanksgiving Day, I sat in the locker room awaiting the opening kickoff of a high-school championship football game. My stomach was churning with pregame nervousness when Claudius strolled into the steaming room. He had given up turkey and dressing with his family and hitchhiked 125 miles to see the game.

After the coach had given the final instructions and we waited in apprehension to take the field, Claudius leaned forward and, with the grin that seemed to split his face in half, said, "Watch them jaybirds when they get the ball. Mean as hell!"

It was enough to send me out free of nervousness and untroubled by the screams of the spectators or the blare of the bands.

When the contest was over, I knelt near the center of the

field, too exhausted, too numb, to move. One eye was red-rimmed with tears, the other already swollen shut and turning blue-black. We had lost, 19-18.

I was oblivious to everything until Claudius slapped my helmet with his palm and said, "It won't be long until people can't even remember who won and who lost. But you keep your score in your own head. You did better than your best today, and that's all you need to remember. The way I figure it, you won."

We walked off the field together, one sweat-stained and beaten, the other striding as if with the champions.

It has been more than two decades since I've seen Claudius or the old Texas cottonwood. It's been that long since I've really listened to the chatter of a mockingbird, or the clatter of a tin can kicked by a bare foot.

But it was only yesterday that I advised a youngster, "Friends don't have to prove nothing to nobody, much less to each other." And it was only today I reminded myself, once again, that "it's just the getting around to doing that scares you, not the doing."

What's more, I still keep my own score in my own head, and that way, a lot of times, I figure I'm a winner.

HOW TO TELL A FRIEND

A questionnaire for fun and to find out about your friends. Simply substitute your friend's name. Score one point for every "yes" answer. All yesses and you have a perfect friendship. But one of the nicest things about friends is that they aren't perfect and don't expect you to be.

	YES	NO
1. Do you know X's telephone number?	☐	☐
2. If you've been out of touch for several months, can you meet without awkwardness?	☐	☐
3. Do you know X's favorite color?	☐	☐
4. Have you ever done anything nice for X without telling him (her) about it?	☐	☐
5. Will X co-sign a loan for you?	☐	☐
6. Has a third party ever regaled you with the admiring stories X tells about you when you're not present?	☐	☐
7. When X can't decide what to drink, does he (she) ask you to pick?	☐	☐
8. Can you list the dishes on X's ideal menu?	☐	☐
9. Can you express angry feelings about each other to each other?	☐	☐
10. Can X make demands on you and vice versa? (What happens if you call X up at 3 A.M.?)	☐	☐
11. Has X ever done anything nice for you even though he (she) stood to suffer for it?	☐	☐
12. If you have a bad back, does X ask you to be careful not to hurt yourself when you are playing tennis?	☐	☐

13. Would you let X have the keys to your house or apartment? ☐ ☐
14. Can you borrow X's car? ☐ ☐
15. When describing a particularly attractive member of the opposite sex to you, does X say, "I know she'd (he'd) really like you"? ☐ ☐
16. Does X remember your birthday? ☐ ☐
17. If X doesn't return your telephone calls, do you feel worried rather than insulted? ☐ ☐
18. Do you know what kind of music X likes best? Dislikes most? ☐ ☐
19. Can you tell X No? ☐ ☐
20. Are you aware of the problem now on X's mind? ☐ ☐
21. Can you list five books X would like to have on a desert island? ☐ ☐
22. Does X tell you when he (she) thinks you're acting like a fool, and you are? ☐ ☐
23. Will X lend you money? Clothes? ☐☐ ☐☐
24. Has X always kept your confidence? ☐ ☐
25. Has X confessed an irrational fear to you? ☐ ☐
26. Do you know what X would like as a birthday present? ☐ ☐
27. Can you spend time together comfortably without talking? ☐ ☐
28. Has X ever brought you chicken soup when you were sick? ☐ ☐
29. Can you say anything that comes into your head when you're with X? ☐ ☐
30. If, contrary to your advice, X marries Y, will he (she) want to retain your friendship? ☐ ☐

FRIENDS: OUR CLOSEST CONNECTION

Some friends arrive all at once, setting off an interior fanfare of immediate recognition. Some arrive slowly, by dint of simple continuity, the accumulation of shared experience gradually stretching to new intimacies. Some arrive dramatically, unexpectedly stepping out from behind a disguise they had previously elaborated. By whatever route they come, friends join us in a kind of conspiracy against the world, circumscribing with us a private space filled with mutual concerns.

TONY JONES

FRIENDSHIP INTERNATIONAL

All friends are strangers at first. Popular writer Jane Howard tells here of a chance encounter with a seatmate. Relive with her the excitement of discovering shared enthusiasms and making a new friend.

I never usually talk to strangers on planes, but Celia Bates, my seatmate on a flight to London, was an exception. We both got up to sit in another section when the movie went on, agreeing that there is something fundamentally wrong about seeing any movie on any plane, and thus began what could become a friendship. It cheers me, as I age, to think that I can have friends fifteen years my junior or, as appeared to be the case with Celia, my senior. It also cheers me to think that somebody I have at this moment never heard of, or only just met, may in a year's time have become important.

Celia's red hair was just beginning to go gray. She had one of those expressive Eleanor Roosevelt faces, a face designed not to stop men in their tracks but to register such of the world's sorrows as it encountered, which in her case had apparently been many, and also to laugh. "Two frightful clichés apply to me," she said as we sipped bloody marys. "I'm 'of a certain age' and 'in reduced circumstances.' " A short marriage, long ago, had been childless, and she had never felt close to her own family in Wilmington, Delaware. She had just returned there "for the last time ever, I hope" for the funeral of her father. For ten years now she had been living on a small inheritance in London, working for a musical publisher only in the mornings so as to have afternoons free for whatever might come up. Once in a while, she said, she thought of looking for more involving work, "but who'd want to hire me at my age? They're all looking for buxom young vixens."

The next afternoon a message in my box at Brown's Hotel said to call Celia. The simple act of phoning made me feel even more euphoric than I had in a morning of blatant materialism on, or rather in, Regent Street. "Have you ever noticed the instructions inside phone booths here?" I asked Celia. " ' . . . wait for continuous purring, dial number or code and number, when you hear rapid pips, press in a coin.' "

"Continuous purring and rapid pips. You see why I don't want to move back to the States?"

"We don't purr as continuously as we might," I had to admit.

"I'm surprised *you've* never lived overseas," Celia later said as we climbed to the upper deck of a bus to Trafalgar Square.

"I was always afraid to leave New York, because I didn't have a nucleus of friends anyplace else. There was this grim image of myself Starting Over on alien turf, away from my loved ones. Shortsighted, maybe, but there you are."

"One Starts Over, as you put it, wherever one is, all the time."

We agreed that the National Portrait Gallery was depressingly filled with compulsive achievers and that museum postcard shops could be as enticing, though this was not a feeling to be proud of, as the original paintings themselves.

Celia invited me to a concert with her and some friends that evening, but for a wonder I had already been asked to dinner in Chelsea.

"So much for my tragic fantasies of existential loneliness in London," I said. "People here are so *nice*."

BEST FRIEND

Stella
appropriately
is fond of
astronomy
takes photographs
of starfish,
and has green stars
for eyes
at home in skies
where tigers walk
on clouds.

LILLIAN MORRISON

THERE IS A SPECIAL BEAUTY ABOUT FRIENDS

Gladys Taber, celebrated cookbook writer and author of books about country life, here discusses our deep need for warm, lasting friendships—people with whom we share our deepest feelings about life, people to whom we are committed. Her words themselves are warm as a February fire.

I grew up in a small town where Father was a college professor, and those colleagues he did not despise often became his intimate friends. And our big living room was a haven for Mama's best friends who brought all their troubles to her. There were couples, too, who were with us on camping trips, picnics, and Sunday afternoon rides. None of us would ever forget the trip to the Dells with the Russells when they had five flat tires and Papa's radiator boiled over. (So did he.)

As for me, I had a best, *best* friend to whom I confided everything, including my desperate love for the football left end. I had a number of others to whom I was deeply devoted, about evenly divided between the girls and the boys. Friends were forever loyal and were expected to be. The worst sin one could commit was to be untrue to a friend, and a few who lacked faithfulness were ostracized rather soon.

Now I try to analyze the change in our lives today. I think as a people we are sociable; in fact, I know a good many men and women who seem frightened to be alone but need the protection of a group most of the time. However cocktail parties, "open house," buffets, barbecues, and dinner parties may ease our insecurity, they cannot substitute for a walk in the sun with a close friend or an evening by the fire with two or three whom we love.

A close, warm friendship is as rugged as a fishing boat going out to the wild sea on a dark day when the tide is high. My own dearest friends do not agree with me on many things, but we can talk about anything and argue and argue, and there is benefit for both sides. For at the core of this relationship is a community of feeling which is basic and has nothing to do with disagreements about politics, going to the moon, or whether we need a new development in the middle of town.

We love and trust a true friend for what he or she is, and living is more enriched by the relationship than words can express. There is in each of us, I think, a deep loneliness, and friendship eases it immeasurably. How sad to think it is growing so scarce nowadays when we need it most.

What does a friendship really mean? In my list, trust, loyalty, and sharing. These are big responsibilities but well worth it. You may tell a true friend anything you wish and be assured it won't be repeated all over town. If you make an unwise remark, it is a stone dropped in a well. The next day someone will *not* call up and say, "I hear you said so and so."

It means your friend is loyal to the relationship and not what used to be called "a summer friend," who faded with the first frost. It also means sharing. It means you are grateful for the privilege of sharing the hard times as well as the glorious ones. If your friend turns to you in trouble, you are really a friend and feel you are worth something special in this troubled world.

There is a special happiness, too, about friends you do not

lose by time or distance. Some of them you may hear from only at Christmas, but the tie is as strong as ever and is one of the brightest aspects of the holiday season. Others may be new friends, and when they come into your life, you feel both an excitement and a sorrow for all the days you missed knowing them.

I would like to feel that friendship will survive as long as mankind inhabits this planet. Sometimes someone says to me, "I don't want to get involved." Or, "I mind my own business and don't depend on anyone." Or, "I am not going to lose my freedom."

This may sound strong and, in a way, noble, but think about the words. We are all involved with one another, whether we accept it or not. We are all born, we all die. We suffer illness. None of us really escapes insecurity at times. We are capable of happiness and love and of loss and longing. We cannot really isolate ourselves from our fellow human beings.

A NEW FRIEND

I found a new friend this very day,
He had a nice smile and a friendly way.

He had red hair and smiling eyes,
And thoughtfulness that was king size.

With him all your worries you would forget,
And his friendliness you'll never regret.

I know I will see him again some day,
And I know that he will be his same pleasant way.

CHERYL BILDERBACK

HOW CHILDREN LEARN TO MAKE FRIENDS

Dr. Benjamin Spock, "the" baby doctor feels friendliness naturally follows a loving upbringing.

Learning friendliness does not really mean learning a set of rules from one's parents like "Be polite to your friends," "Share your toys," "Do what your visitor wants to do, not what you want to do," though parents often do have to give such reminders.

Friendliness is basically a love of other people, an enjoyment of them and a spontaneous desire to please them. It comes most fundamentally from the fact that we are social beings, ready to love company if things go right in our development.

The development of our sociability has to be given a good head start by our having parents who are delighted with us in infancy, who smile at us, hug us, talk baby talk to us. Then, after the age of one or two, the warmth engendered in us by our parents turns increasingly outward to other people—adults and children.

HOW DO YOU GET A FRIEND?

*A children's story answers the question—you just say
"hello." Then you do something together. And it's exactly
the same for grown-ups!*

Sally's friends were far away.
They lived near Sally's old house.

Sally did not have friends here.
"How can I get a friend?" she wondered.
"How can I get someone to play with?"

Sally sat on the back step.
She looked into the next yard.
A little boy was playing there.
He had a lot of boxes.
Some boxes were big.
Some boxes were little.
He had crayons.
He took a big box.
He made some windows on it with a red crayon.
He made a door with a brown crayon.
He made the box look like a house.

"I wish I could play with him," said Sally.
"I wish I could make a box look like a house.
How can I be his friend?"

The little boy looked up.
He saw Sally.
He smiled at her.

"Hello," said Sally.
"May I play with you?
You make the boxes look nice."

Sally and Mike began to play.
They took a tall box.
They made many windows on it.
"It looks like a big house in the city," said Sally.
They took a little box.
They made one big window on it.
"It looks like a store," said Mike.

Soon they were friends.

"I wanted to know how to get a friend,"
said Sally to her mother that night.
"Now I know how.
You just say hello."

SHEILA K. HOLLANDER

A SPRIG OF MINT FOR ALLEN

Katherine Anne Porter, famous novelist and essayist, offers her love and best wishes to a young-spirited old friend on his birthday.

A sixtieth birthday is impressive, what the Mexicans call *una bola de años*, a ball of years; it represents a triumph of durability and vitality, and at least a partial victory of the spirit in what turned out, after all, to be a pretty long war. I am particularly impressed when it occurs to someone I have known since he was twenty-seven years old, already a poet of great gifts and a critic of severe and obstinate character—I mean by that, with his caliber of mind, a good critic. Ah well, here he is, and how did he get here? I am reminded again that, though a year is added to my life every twelve months, and every year in the sweet month of May I celebrate with love and praise the recklessness of my father and mother, I cannot budge the friends of my youth out of *their* youth in my mind and heart: there they remain in a frame of light with a backdrop of blue sky and green field—it does not occur to me that anybody is getting older except myself. I am not taking it very hard, either, not speeding it up unnecessarily—there is all the time in the world.

So, as for my friend Allen Tate, I know well he is a grandfather and has been one for a great while, but it happened to him so early he was the youngest grandfather I ever knew personally. It did nothing to age him in my eyes. When some of John Crowe Ransom's friends, Allen among them, invited me to Mr. Ransom's sixtieth birthday party, I thought it quite all right, very natural for him, because I had never seen him when he was younger; yet even then I felt that sixty is a little young to begin giving testimonials and memorials and getting our special numbers of magazines. It might put notions in a man's head about getting old. So I delight in the spectacle of our dear John Crowe Ransom, how successfully he has resisted all the well-meaning, admiring attempts of his misguided loving friends to embalm him while he is still walking around thinking live thoughts.

I am, as you see, against the whole project of making a production of Allen's sixtieth birthday; he is simply not old enough yet, he still has much to do. I nearly made it, not quite as usual, to Robert Frost's eightieth birthday party. That is more like it. A great poet who survives in his powers to that age should be given a public vote of thanks and all the honors lying around loose at the time. But Allen cannot be called venerable by any stretch of the word and he shouldn't be summed up at this point. If you plan to give a gay birthday party with plenty of champagne and music and dancing and flowers, do invite me. I may not get there, but I'd like being invited. Let's not be solemn about the passing of time and the reputations of our literary men. Allen's is safe, I think—let's let him live and grow. It is splendid to think another good poet has lived to be sixty years old, for the real ones do grow in grace as they go on—I am remembering Hardy, Yeats, Frost, Eliot—so I wish my old friend joy of his years in health and just the right degree of disturbance, upset, uproar, and controversy that he can best thrive on to write his poetry. Many happy returns of the day, with my love.

Beauty, who creates
All sweet delights for men,
Brings honor at will, and makes the false seem true
Time and again.

(PINDAR)

Children's poems express some of the basic joys of friendship: being together, holding a hand in the dark, getting along in spite of an occasional fight, and the sink-in-the-stomach feeling when a friend moves away.

FRIENDS

On Saturday,
No matter the weather,
The three of us
Will get together
And play whatever
We want to play,
And wish all week
Was Saturday.

D.J. ALLAN

THE DARK

It's not so dark
when evening falls—
if you are close
to me.
It's only dark
when I am caught
without a hand
to squeeze.

PATRICIA SKARRY

HOW COME?

Why is it that
when I'm angry with Philip Hyena
my whole day
seems bad?
And why is it
when we've settled the fight
my whole day seems to go
perfectly right?

LEE BENNETT HOPKINS

SANDRA MOVED AWAY

Last year I had a little chum,
And oh, such fun all day.
Then came a great big trailer
truck—
And Sandra moved away.

ETHEL MAE PAUL

COMMON ELEMENTS

All I do is look about me, mark those to whom I feel I am a friend and note what it is I feel. I cannot even be sure the relationship is mutual. I may know I am X's friend; X may not agree that he is mine. In some cases I will never know. Lovers enjoy reiterating their feeling for each other; friends rarely do so.

What do I feel about my few friendships? Can I distinguish any elements common to all of them? Perhaps half a dozen or so.

1. *Admiration.* This is an absolute. Each friend has some large quality or qualities that mean a great deal to me, and in which he is my superior. But not excessively. Somewhere in one of his confessional works André Gide remarks that he was always uneasy when he visited his friend Paul Valéry, because Valéry's mind was so much more subtle and rapid than his own. The discrepancy must be there; but it must not be an abyss. And the admiration must be a two-way street.

2. *Community.* My friend and I must share a common interest—and that interest must have scope and depth. According to some theorists, the common interest may be trivial: golf, television, stamp-collecting, the Democratic or Republican Party. I have not found it so. I suspect locker-room friendships, indeed all hobby friendships; their base is rickety.

3. *Taken-for-grantedness.* We do not have to explain, defend, excuse ourselves. Friendship emerges from liking only after the friend is accepted as *given.* Here it diverges from the romantic phase of love, one of whose exquisite pleasures flows from mutual, continuous (and repetitious) self-explanation. One measure of friendship consists not in the number of things friends can discuss, but in the number of things they need no longer mention.

4. *Purposelessness*. Thoreau had the happy faculty of saying deep things about matters he knew little of. Thus: "The most I can do for my friend is simply to be his friend." That is perfect. I can understand what antiquity would have called "appetitive" love; but friendship is purposeless, or should be. It merely *is*. I reject the notion that the critical test of a friend is whether he would help you in a jam. Some people are good in jams; others poor. It is a specialized talent, like marksmanship. Too many *acts* of friendship, particularly those excessive ones we call acts of self-sacrifice, may endanger the relationship. One should not have to be overgrateful to a friend. The sense of obligation and the sense of guilt are neighbors. Perfect friends owe each other nothing but themselves.

5. *Ambivalence*. A repulsive mode-word, but perhaps apt to our discussion. In Pamela Hansford Johnson's novel, *An Error of Judgment*, Victor Hendrey remarks: "Dislike and friendship are not mutually exclusive, I have found out for myself time and time again." This is of our time; and it is true. Unremitting mutual benevolence may have been characteristic of ideal classical friendship. It seems inapposite today. One *should* dislike one's friends at times, and be prepared to be disliked by them. An infusion of irony, though never of recrimination, helps keep friendship fresh, sweet and sharp. In heaven, we are told, there is no marriage. Nor is there any friendship. Saints are incapable of friendship. In heaven I should seek out saints only as mentors; and here on earth I do not seek them out as friends. I am lucky in my friends, for they, like me, are rich in faults, and the ironical perception of these faults is a necessary ingredient in our relationship.

6. *Selfishness.* Friendship is an exclusive condition. There can be a circle of friends, but its circumference is limited. "Everybody's friend," says Schopenhauer, "is nobody's." A saint can give himself to all. A joiner can give himself to all. But a friend is an amiable snob, and I prize his exclusiveness, for it enhances me. The man who invites you to meet his friends, who turn out to be fifty couples, may be an excellent host and a charming fellow, but you will pass the evening without discovering whether or not he is capable of friendship. "He who is the friend of all humanity," says one of Molière's characters, "is not my friend."

I have isolated six qualities that appear to be common to my few, not numerous friendships. They are not qualities the great theorists of friendship would have stressed. They are merely a few (the ability to talk well might be another; I do not understand silent friendships) that I can isolate from my own small experience, and which therefore are probably to be found elsewhere among my contemporaries.

CLIFTON FADIMAN

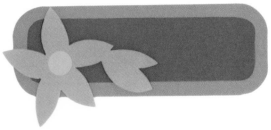

BE YOUR OWN FRIEND FIRST

In their runaway best-seller, HOW TO BE YOUR OWN BEST FRIEND, psychologists Mildred Newman and Bernard Berkowitz make the point that real self-love is the root of real friendship; we must care for ourselves before we can cherish others. Their words are well worth pondering.

Doing what makes you feel good about yourself is really the opposite of self-indulgence. It doesn't mean gratifying an isolated part of you; it means satisfying your whole self, and this includes the feelings and ties and responsibilities you have to others, too. Self-indulgence means satisfying the smallest part of you, and that only temporarily.

It does mean being self-centered enough to care for yourself and to take care of yourself. If you don't learn how to do that, you can never care properly for others. The Bible says, "Love thy neighbor *as* thyself," not "better than" or "instead of" thyself. If we cannot love ourselves, where will we draw our love for anyone else? People who do not love themselves can adore others, because adoration is making someone else big and ourselves small. They can desire others, because desire comes out of a sense of inner incompleteness, which demands to be filled. But they cannot love others, because love is an affirmation of the living, growing being in all of us. If you don't have it, you can't give it.

In some respects friends are like surprise packages: you can never be quite sure what's hidden in the outer wrappings. But more than that, there's a challenge implicit in the starting of a friendship that doesn't exist in most other personal relationships. After all, you inherit your family, you're assigned to your classmates, you acquire your neighbors by chance. But a friend you *choose* to be with; and she chooses you in return. The fact is that a friend is often the first person in your life who isn't *required* to like you.

NORMAN LOBSENZ

FRIEND

A warm handclasp,
    A fond embrace,
A friendly smile
    When face to face—
A cheerful greeting
    Which seems to say
That you're concerned
    This makes my day.

I sense a gladness
    When we meet
Upon the stair
    Or on the street.
Your sparkling eye—
    This simple act
Makes glad my heart,
    Now, that's a fact.

LOUIS EVERETT DOWNING

Acknowledgments

The editor and the publisher have made every effort to trace the ownership of all copyrighted material and to secure permission from copyright holders of such material. In the event of any question arising as to the use of any material the publisher and editor, while expressing regret for inadvertent error, will be pleased to make the necessary corrections in future printings. Thanks are due to the following authors, publishers, publications and agents for permission to use the material indicated.

CURTIS-BROWN LTD., for "How Come?" by Lee Bennett Hopkins.

CHAPPELL MUSIC COMPANY, for excerpt from "Friendship" from *Du Barry Was A Lady* by Cole Porter, copyright © 1939 by Chappell & Co. Inc., renewed.

KATHERINE NELSON DAVIS for "A Tribute to a Friend."

DELACORTE PRESS/SEYMOUR LAWRENCE, for "A Spring of Mint for Allen" from *The Collected Essays and Occasional Writings of Katherine* Anne Porter, copyright © 1970 by Katherine Anne Porter.

DOUBLEDAY & COMPANY, INC., for "Heart Friends" from *Who Am I, God?* by Marjorie Holmes, copyright © 1970, 1971 by Marjorie Holmes Mighell; for "How To Be a Collector's Item" from *Please Don't Eat the Daisies* by Jean Kerr, copyright © 1956 by Jean Kerr.

E. P. DUTTON & CO. INC., for excerpt from *A Different Woman* by Jane Howard, copyright © 1973 by Jane Howard.

CLIFTON FADIMAN, for excerpt from his article which appeared in the June 1967 issue of Holiday.

GARRARD PUBLISHING COMPANY, for "Friends" by D. J. Allen, from *Hello People*, copyright 1972 by Leland B. Jacobs.

HARCOURT BRACE JOVANOVICH INC., for excerpt from *The Four Loves*, by C. S. Lewis, copyright © 1960 by Helen Joy Lewis.

HARPER'S, for excerpt from *Friends: Making the Connection* by Tony Jones; for *How to Tell a Friend from an Acquaintance*, copyright © 1973 by Harper's Magazine, reprinted by permission from August 1973 issue.

HAWTHORN BOOKS, for excerpt from *Men, Women and Cats* by Dorothy Van Doren, copyright © 1960 by Dorothy Van Doren.

HIGHLIGHTS FOR CHILDREN, INC., for "How Do You Get a Friend?" by Sheila K. Hollander, copyright © 1969 by Highlights for Children, Inc; for "Sandra Moved Away" by Ethel Mae Paul, copyright © 1972 by Highlights for Children, Inc.

ROBERT LESCHER LITERARY AGENCY, for excerpt from article by Dr. Benjamin Spock which appeared in *Redbook*, November 1972, copyright © 1973 by John D. Houston II, Trustee under an irrevocable Trust agreement dated January 5, 1970, between Benjamin M. Spock, Donor and John D. Houston II, Trustee; for excerpt from "The Value of Friendship" by Norman Lobsenz, copyright © 1971 by Triangle Communications, Inc., reprinted from November 1971 issue of *Seventeen*.

J. B. LIPPINCOTT COMPANY, for excerpt from *Country Chronicle* by Gladys Taber, copyright © 1974 by Gladys Taber.

LITTLE, BROWN AND COMPANY, for excerpt from *An Unfinished Woman: A Memoir* by Lillian Hellman, copyright © 1969 by Lillian Hellman.

LILLIAN MORRISON, for "Best Friend" from *Miranda's Music*, copyright © 1968 by Lillian Morrison.

THE NEW AMERICAN LIBRARY, INC., for "Fix-Up" from *It's Hard to be Hip Over Thirty* by Judith Viorst, copyright © 1968 by Judith Viorst.

RANDOM HOUSE, INC., for excerpt from *How To Be Your Own Best Friend* by Mildred Newman and Bernard Berkowitz with Jean Owen, copyright © 1971 by Mildred Newman and Bernard Berkowitz.

READER'S DIGEST, for "Yonder's My Best Friend" by Rob Wood, The Reader's Digest, September 1968, copyright 1968 by The Reader's Digest Assn., Inc.

PATRICIA SKARRY RUTTER for "The Dark."

Illustrated by Eulala Conner
Designed by Caitlin Michaels
Set in Century Expanded
Printed by Federated Lithograph
Printed on Chatfield Rainbow Offset